LOADERS

Amanda Askew

FIREFLY BOOKS

A FIREFLY BOOK

Published by Firefly Books Ltd. 2010

First printing

Publisher Cataloging-in-Publication Data (U.S.)
Askew, Amanda.
   Mighty machines : loaders / Amanda Askew.
[24] p. : col. photos. ; cm. (Mighty machines)
Includes index.
Summary: Includes loaders shoveling snow, loaders on building sites and loaders fixing roads.
ISBN-13: 978-1-55407-706-9 (pbk.)
ISBN-10: 1-55407-706-0 (pbk.)
1. Excavating machinery -- Juvenile literature. 2. Loaders (Machines) -- Juvenile literature.
I. Title.
[E] 624.1/52 dc22   TA735.A77 2010

Library and Archives Canada Cataloguing in Publication
Askew, Amanda
        Loaders / Amanda Askew.
(Mighty machines)
Includes index.
ISBN-13: 978-1-55407-706-9 (pbk.)
ISBN-10: 1-55407-706-0 (pbk.)
        1. Loaders (Machines)--Juvenile literature.
2. Earthmoving machinery--Juvenile literature.
I. Title. II. Series: Mighty machines (Richmond Hill, Ont.)
TA725.A85 2010   j621.8'65   C2010-901149-X

Published in the United States by
Firefly Books (U.S.) Inc.
P.O. Box 1338, Ellicott Station
Buffalo, New York 14205

Published in Canada by
Firefly Books Ltd.
66 Leek Crescent
Richmond Hill, Ontario L4B 1H1

Manufactured by 1010 Printing International Ltd. in Huizhou, Guangdong, China in May 2010, Job # JQ10010485.

Written by Amanda Askew
Designed by Phil and Traci Morash (Fineline Studios)
Editor Angela Royston
Picture Researcher Maria Joannou

Associate Publisher Zeta Davies
Editorial Director Jane Walker

Words in **bold** can be found in the Glossary on page 23.

Contents

What is a **loader?**

Loaders are tractors with a large bucket on the front. They scoop up earth or **rubble** and load it onto trucks to be taken away.

Loaders can drive on the road to get from one building site to another.

Loaders are used mainly on **building sites**. Loaders usually have wheels. They can move around the building site more quickly than other machines.

A loader picks up the earth, instead of pushing it along the ground like a **bulldozer** does.

Parts of a loader

A loader has three main parts — a cab, a bucket and the **booms**. The bucket is attached to the booms. The bucket carries the earth and rubble.

The driver sits in the cab to control the loader. He lifts the bucket by moving the booms.

tractor

bucket

cab

wheel

boom

The wheels of a loader have deep grooves, or treads, to help them grip the ground.

Buckets and claws

The bucket is usually wide and **rectangular**. It has teeth along the bottom to help it to scoop up things on the ground.

The bucket can be changed for other tools. For example, a loader with a giant claw can pick up logs of wood.

The boom and claw on this loader are bending over backwards to pick up the logs!

The bucket is a large scoop at the front of the tractor.

Mines and quarries

Loaders that work in **mines** and **quarries** are called front loaders, or bucket loaders. They have a very large bucket on the front of the machine.

The loader tips coal into the back of a truck.

WA 450

Front loaders can move big piles of coal, stones and other things. They load the coal onto trucks. The trucks take the coal to where it is needed.

The conveyor belt moves stones into a large pile ready for the loader.

In the Snow

Front loaders work well in snow. Their wheels don't slip, even on icy ground. Loaders can quickly clear snow from roads or pavements.

The bucket scoops up the snow and carries it away. Loaders work at airports, too. They clear snow from the **runways**.

When the loader has cleared the runway of snow, the planes will be able to take off again.

This loader has chains around its wheels to stop it slipping.

13

Mending roads

Backhoe loaders are used for mending roads. The tractor is small and it has an extra bucket on the back. This bucket is used for digging.

The small bucket breaks up the ground using its teeth. The large bucket scoops up the pieces and loads them onto a **dump truck**.

The driver can face the front or the back to use the large or small bucket.

The bucket at the back is called the backhoe.

In small spaces

A skid loader is much smaller than a normal loader. It is sometimes used instead of a **digger** in small spaces. For example, it can work underneath a building.

The small bucket can carry and load material. It can also push earth along the ground.

A skid loader doesn't need a lot of room to work. It can turn all the way around, while staying on the same spot!

The loader can lift the bucket up very high, using the long booms.

On the farm

Loaders can move **bales** of hay and **straw**. The bucket is taken off and a long spike is put on instead. The spike is called a bale spear.

The loader spikes a bale of hay and then lifts it up.

The bale spear can have one spike or many spikes. Some spikes are longer than others. Two long spikes are needed to lift big, heavy bales of hay.

This tractor has one strong boom at the side.

Biggest and smallest

The biggest loader in the world has a bucket that could carry 88 tons in one scoop. That's the same weight as 13 elephants.

The bucket is so tall that an adult can stand up inside it!

20

Small skid loaders are only about 35 inches wide — that is just more than three of these books laid end to end! They can be used inside farm buildings.

This farmer is using a skid loader to clear away dirty straw.

Activities

- Here are three loaders from the book. Can you remember what they do?

- If you needed to lift a bale of hay, which loader would you choose. Why did you choose that loader?

- Draw a loader moving large piles of earth. Which loader did you choose? What color is it? Who is driving it?

- Which picture shows a backhoe loader?

Glossary

Bale
A large block of hay or straw that is tied together.

Boom
A long arm. A loader's booms hold the bucket.

Building site
A place where a house or other building is being built.

Bulldozer
A tractor with a blade on the front. It is used to push earth and rubble.

Digger
A digger is a machine that digs holes.

Dump truck
A truck with a large container on the back that tilts to dump earth and rubble onto the ground.

Mine
A deep hole in the ground. Coal is often found in a mine.

Quarry
A place where stone and sand are dug out of the ground.

Rectangular
Shaped with two long sides and two short sides.

Rubble
Broken stones or bricks, usually on a building site.

Runway
Part of an airport where airplanes take off and land.

Straw
The dried stems of plants, such as wheat or oats.

Index